D1236497

* * * Judge Citation

"So who is this healing really for?" wonders one poem in this collection full of wondering and wonderment, this constellation of poems spilling over with the vast aches of a heart so attuned to life, loss, and more life. To step into the world of to be in & of is to understand the in's and of's that shape an ever-shifting Black queer existence and imagination—how a preposition can be a position, a perspective, a power: imposed or em-braced, relived or revised. To step into the gorgeous, dizzying cosmos of this chapbook is to declare "we're raunchy, we're righteous," to sing "we kissed, & for weeks nothing was my enemy," and ultimately, to "invent a galaxy of sound."

—**Chen Chen**, Guest Judge for the 2022 Palette Poetry Chapbook Prize, author of *Your Emergency Contact Has Experienced an Emergency* and *When I Grow Up I Want to Be a List of Further Possibilities*

* * * Praise for **to be in & of** * * *

"*to be in & of.* To be verb & noun. To be object & subject. To be Black & blue. Joshua Aiken is contemplating & exploding all the dichotomies in this tight collection of poems, putting pressure on language like he means to turn each word into coal & then burn it all down. But don't be deceived: there's a phoenix rising from these ashes—& ready to fly."

—**Evie Shockley**, author of *Suddenly We*

"What is there to say? These poems are excellent, lyrically athletic, brazenly honest, as sound as they are shattering. They move through you like winter wind, mark you like a cloudless summer day. As I read I found myself shouting or stunned silent after every poem. Joshua Aiken, how you see and feel the world in these poems, how you witness your life and life around you, is nothing short of genius. Reader, beware: here awaits a brutal and lush vision in which you too, naked and human, might also be glimpsed."

—**Danez Smith**, author of *Homie*

to be in
& of

Poems by Joshua Aiken

Winner of the 2022 Palette Poetry Chapbook Prize

Published in the United States of America by Palette Poetry
www.palettepoetry.com

ISBN 979-8-9882557-2-7

Cover design by Emelie Mano.
Book design by Julianne Johnson.

Cover artwork:
Mark Fleuridor
Overwhelming then Silent #3
Ink, Archival Glue and Collage on Watercolor Paper
~22.5" x 21.5"
2023

In this series of pieces titled *"Overwhelming then Silent"* the artist created collaged moments out of his mother praying. The artist remembers viewing his mother in moments of vulnerability where she would weep while praying. He often thinks about the release of emotions prayer may provide someone and uses these pieces to depict that emotional state. An Overwhelming rise of emotion but then Silence after.

Disappearing Act

who did what   *when*   */when /*   *how why* sings
the owl strutting on the pavement.   *how*

did it happen? mumbled words   from   alabaster
stones, crumbled limbs of bodies chewed but not understood.

when my parents call, tell me *baby someone shot Carlton*
/ Carlton's dead / how the world spins.   truly, its axes

listen closely and gravity does its work and, truly, we have
learned, how irrational it is that each gust of   wind knows

the funeral hymn too. so first, i found the picture Jonovan took:
you at the grand canyon, the gutted canvas   where you wrote *da world*

spin. second, i ripped every track from your   soundcloud page
before it's taken down, because us & the defying birds always knew

the sound of bullets because—*Isaac*,   because—we love flying
falling things. music—like you, like me—stays about him: disappearing

before the seconds act. each final thing is this: Lord   knows,
it is what is for you that is done to me. this life. this passive

voice, how putrid the lie. i'm tired. /   things / don't just happen
for a reason. black helical beauts atop your infant head, pawing

figures which first reached out from auntie's womb: *this earth*
so loved her that you happened and you (and you) were   borne

and, indeed, made. your / taking / yes,   ensnaring, yes, stealing
yes, impoverishing / of life /it was done, and no reasons suffice.

no reasons good. instead just crows. just a nest. just twigs
& planets. places to place / our love /   & you &

                     you / & /

Sovereignty

All my registers say *hush*

A spider pushes each ounce of knowledge against the ground
Her hydraulic soldiers

I hear wind scurrying through the walls

The night prior I had looked in the mirror
Felt a splashing wound open up inside of me

Pressure Pressure is the only thing I think to feel

The spider climbs the glass-shoulder
of a bottle of wine My liquid lobotomy

I keep asking for God
                    Tinkering my skepticism
Grating my sense of self
into a bowl

Little guardian of dusty apartment floors
has danced herself a lurid nest

And she did it so quietly

Leftovers, pt. 1

& give me the fatback & the husbands who left [ding]

the husbands & the child [ding] there never could be &

the bridge where he [ding] & this—that *nothing's ever ready,*

we just say things to bear what time decides—is where we keep

the grief & the grief doesn't & grandmama did [ding] eat

fistfuls of cornstarch in her bedroom [ding] so it started

to feel small & even though [ding] i barely knew him i'm told

we [ding] look alike [ding] so i think i know granddad's absence well

& it's the summer i gain forty pounds [ding] when knowing most hurts &

i'm sober smell not of hospital & michelle flushed the pills [ding] i set the timer

to breath—*four, seven, eight*—in lieu of knifing my wrists [ding] & yet i'm barren

life [ding] not new [ding] live from the disciple's table & starved [ding]

& *i'm not sure i'm getting better* [ding] & my family does not eat [ding] in excess

we eat & fill what's missing with ourselves & is this not [ding] violence

[ding] & its afterlife [ding] & *a microwave, a headlock, a spanking,* [ding] *a do you remember*

& [ding] is this not how [ding] we get through life [ding] by taking [ding] killing

[ding] into our own hands & [ding] *wash them before you*

& forgive [ding] & get the collard greens

[ding] wet with summer & bacon's grease

The Trouble With Angels

"We need, in every community, a group of angelic troublemakers. Our power is in our ability to make things unworkable. The only weapon we have are our bodies...we need to tuck them in places so the wheels don't turn."
- Bayard Rustin

rub an empty pistol and beg it
for a wish: piecemeal this casket
back into that tree. then swallow
their Mississippi whole. admit that
where is just another war. thus
black, our queer; thus, blood
you left here—*& yet that face*
still has your name.
the rowboat and that river.
what they couldn't steal.

tell me about the ghost that didn't
drown. show them no closet, sprig
no splintered door. tell us
what you learned dying and living
twice. kiss everything you are
told to kill.

*** **IN** ***

I Lied When I Said I Never Have Dreams

after Richard Siken

1. In this one, I die in a car. Rain comes down like pearls, the sky jabs punches
   at the earth, and the sports-utility-vehicle goes a little too fast. There is a boy
   who I could say I slept with and regret, but would rather say there was just
   a boy. Do we not all have this dream? The one with death and he
   who pushed you closer to it? One where you promise: If I survive
   this, I'll never take from the pomegranate tree again.

2. I crash. I crash and the game is over and the blood has won
   and I'm telling the truth this time. So spit in your hand and let's
   shake. Please? *Honey, please?*

3. In this dream, our mothers meet. It is then, in a barren
   chapel, with a casket covered in hydrangeas. They are telling
   stories that rest behind our ears, reminders we are more than just
   boys. One of us plays dead.

4. Here, I die in a car driving home from prom. This dream was
   true once and it was not me or my body but it was a boy
   who I imagine was like me and who I imagine had not
   suffocated just yet and I thus envied him so. That's what all the end
   -less tears are about. The car, the lurid moon, the night I cannot
   resist putting myself in.

5. It's a different car this time. You're driving. Say, a Honda Accord.
   I hear that black cars are the most likely to crash—says I, the black boy,
   to the boy I love. Tendril vines for fingers, we lean in and kiss.
   The dream zooms in on the rearview mirror and you can see
   our paired skulls, gracefully framed, by the headlights coming our way.

6. *"[T]he threshold test indicates that black and Hispanic drivers were searched on the basis of less evidence
   than white drivers. We assessed racial disparities in policing in the United States...analyzing a dataset detail
   -ing nearly 100 million traffic stops...[w]e found that black drivers were less likely to be stopped after
   sunset, when a 'veil of darkness' masks one's race, suggesting bias in stop decision."*

7. This time, the black boy dies. There is no car, and if there is one
   the seatbelt must be long as it is (to be used as) a noose. If there is
   a car, it does not go too fast as the parade route is not long in this town.
   I die because someone will kill me and my mother will cry
   and tomorrow breakfast will taste exactly the same.

8. This time, the black boy dies. Maybe there's a car, maybe a gun,
   maybe a hotel room, and maybe another crumpled body in the street.
   These dreams are mine; don't forget.

9. I die because I crash into a deer. Poor thing.
   All it gets to be is added to a list of casualties and a list of dreams.

10. In this dream, I am the deer. And I am so in love.
    Those eyes. The damn headlight eyes God gave you.

11. I am hit by a car. I do not lie there, but rather truth.
    I do not die there, I am simply dying. There is no bright light.
    It could be a fire truck or a steam engine or a tank or
    a police car or a plow or a brick wall or a chained-to-
    a-fence something or any other way our bodies are disposed.

12. In this dream, I am shot in the back. I look
    over my brazen shoulder and dramatically say: *You're lucky
    someone else didn't beat you to it.*

13. In this dream, there was no one. I promise babe, *no one!* Well there was
    that woman on TV who used antifreeze to kill her husband, but besides that.

14. There was just me and my unnamed pain that I nurtured
    like a pet. Me in the garage. Me pouring myself a tall glass
    of something not-so-nice. In this dream, empty was just
    a feeling and not the boy who kissed your neck.

15. This time, I die in bed. Not mine. The boy I
    never loved is a corpse in tall man's clothes. The boy I
    did not even really like has given me something to help me
    sleep—and now, clutches my side. Death's touch feels
    like sniffles and a cold. The boy did not leave. This
    is when the dreams stop or maybe where they start. I
    press rewind. The fast forward button disappears.

16. I die in my own bed.

17. A plane crash.

18. The day after my mother. Caskets made
    of a pomegranate tree. We both peek out and look
    around. She whispers: *We can be so loved and still die so easy.*

19. This time no one. I do
    not die. Not mother. Not you. Death
    stays home sick. Poor thing.

20. Not a nightmare. Just another jeweled surrender at night.

[A]bsence is an [A]xiom

call my tongue a snout
& my body will : i will eat
i will : but i won't : stop
making the same : scar
twice : sorry : that's too
bloody a scene : there's no
villain in this play : give me
a name and i'll sing :
here's the lonely deal
my body is where it's not
here's the not : my body is
inside itself and clawing at
the wounds : here's the knot :
here's what i can't : call my
liver a liver : and i'll know
everyone sitting at the bar :
call my lung a lung and i'll
have the whole pack : these
are conjectures not truths :
remember i eat : i starve :
gorge: i lunge : i be : for the
slop : i look for the mess : that
is me : here's the deal : the
tame beast : fills a void : the
white space : grabs me : the
pup's affirmed command : is
me : the loud bark : the sealed
mouth : i be : i be

Scorpions in Bethesda

Scorpions are small thirty-five pound "precision" glide bombs "probably no bigger than a violin case" used by the Central Intelligence Agency.

Under the Obama Administration the use of drone strikes were significantly increased, claiming a significant reduction in civilian killings. The Administration used an estimation method that involved "count[ing] all military-age males in a strike zone as combatant...unless there is explicit intelligence posthumously proving them innocent."

calling a hole -- a home -- is to murmur
-- in morse code -- is -- to reject --
the scattering of a place -- to cough up
debris -- far away firewood is a tickling
mother -- firewood just a frightening
ghost -- death just the aftermath -- the
unaccompanied result -- if you crawl
from underneath x you must be within
-- or subsumed -- by x. it follows --
one could say -- that an ordered strike
-- from a drone -- invokes the feeling
-- that comes -- after kissing -- a child
goodnight. dangerous particles -- x
must accept -- might graze y's skin
-- before -- the world -- turns bright
again. it -- comes with -- the territory
-- it being -- violence -- it being --
the forest floor. venom is a healing
substance. it -- the subject of our
bodies -- is the re-armor -- it -- the
generous poison -- saves us -- from
ourselves -- it -- the bare life -- relies
-- on the notion -- that -- the shepherd
clothed -- us too. my empty -- nest
-- burdened -- above -- holds a knitted
blanket -- my destructed -- is casted
-- lesser evil -- my destructed -- is
not -- made of -- my brothers' limbs
-- my destructed -- is -- not the same
-- but the shell. if death -- be in my

name -- what explodes -- but -- the
baseball bat -- grandpa beget -- the
rubber tires -- beneath -- my mother's
oiled dragon -- barreling -- across turtle
island -- and the beetles -- the bison --
the violins singing -- "mercy" -- all
while -- all the while. there are inflamed
-- arachnids -- piercing – *Pakistan. (Yemen?*
Somalia? Afghanistan?) -- the frightened
-- thundered -- unsound -- sky.

to love through what scares you

let's drive somewhere because
when i try to be the boy who
does beautiful under the moonlight
glow of a steak & shake, i always
begin in tears & end up reviving
some buried bad feeling that i know
is nestled up close with one
of the ones i want to recall. ones
that i want to crawl back in me
& to save me from the country of men
who smear their spit
& blur truth
in order to   blow
the heads off despair
all in the name
of not sanity but safety. whose?
never mine. safety being that which i try
on whenever a man or a bruise gives
me anything & so
in my dreams i do everything but try it.
in my dreams i call my mother routinely
i quit my job & drive
past the gone-by down-sun towns
& their lines drawn in the
past-present sand & just before
the willing
fertile ground, i stop
en route,
because i want bad food
& corporate soda to
laugh-cry into, just in case
love is just a person
who stands in for forgiveness
but actually comes through—
because it's high-time we
got what we were looking for.
if i know anything it's that
what's holy sits next to what scares
the right-wing of the eagle

& the left-brain of you.
you can seek sanctuary but this is
everything, this is everything that the
age of tv dinners killed but can't undo.
this is the only buried promise,
which the smell of grease
comes past the counter & covers up,
but us sweaty can't-grow-ups who must spoon-
feed ourselves myths to stay alive; we catch our own replies:

drive
drive fast
drive fast toward skylines
fast toward skylines kissed by a lip
color called joy

Demand

Slapping my   palms   on the pavement
when   no gold coin   ever appears.

Skunking   my face inside out constantly. Glory
running the day   nobody must   see me for me to be me.

I'll begin   without   a beginning:
I didn't want   to be here   to begin with.

No, I've   been   an epistemic catastrophe.
I've asked   him   to knock me out,   to run me over.

I've asked   to watch   as he does. I've asked
to be nothing   —my blue-wish of anticipation—

done this   as to be   a proxy   for his
care.   I am a rickety vessel.

A seaborne surrender. I've asked   to be this everywhere
as grocery stores   in this world   are loud oceans too.

All I've wanted   is to paint every   TV screen
black   and thrust my fist   through the glass.

Now I long   to play my life: minus errant scenes
without   all this produce   up for sale.

Me?   I'll pick up   the joystick.
I'll weather   every encounter   if it means

not having   to sit and stay. I'm seeking
excess.   I'm wanting   more.

Wanting some other universe   where I do
more   than seek   and hide and bleed.

Hunger ("While I Wait, I'm the Only Man Who Loves Me")

after "Homocide" by Essex Hemphill

I spent my grief on you, but fault myself for making of everything
a currency. I fixed myself underneath a STOP sign in the rain,

but I was in your arms, feckless, because someone I love was dead
again. This time even the funeral was too far away. Distance

always a metric of distinction; me readily lost in your chest,
your breathing, crumpled, as you offered to carry me home.

It was mackerel, prawn, monkfish—a menu—before my eyes
after I told you *I'm good, but should eat.* I told you, *I can't be*

an experiment, & we kissed, & for weeks nothing was my enemy.
You'd come home sweaty from sport & cook peanut stew,

& we'd take turns being weary, you of prescription and divinity,
me of my fingernails, the pitch of my voice, of how easy I am to win.

I don't know what you needed or need, but I smoked menthols,
spilled whiskey, lied to everyone, made of my mourning a stage, a stature,

condition, a state: the prized jewel wants in between
our knees, won't take me headless—I'm useful, I'm discreet.

Listen, I forgive me. You loved me in sorrow, love sorrowed,
& I loved sorrow eagerly. I needed a place to be. A harpoon doesn't

wait for a squid to get lonely. I spent months there, in bed with your window
open, unsure of the day. In practice, you're kind & so am I

thus, we're prone to being prudishly cruel. I was. I am. Familiar with,
not undone, by men who precisely want me

off my feet.

Leftovers, pt. 2

& my college therapist says *not that many people die of natural causes* [ding]

four funerals that i managed [ding] to attend in twenty-two months &

even a classmate springs [ding] to correct me [ding] *well, hypertension doesn't "run"*

in families & mind you [ding] both of them were black & [ding] i was

with them [ding] i was in it & at the funeral the dessert was brought by [ding]

the middle-aged white folks i was staring at & my cousin's cousin explains the [ding]

white babies grandmommy brought up & they brought apple-cobbler &

[ding] the black boys that killed isaac are behind bars [ding] & america is not

[ding] & it is quiet [ding] at the table of complicity & guilt & *you're still in*

school? & you're still in school? & with whom [ding] do i socratic method

what's roosting [ding] in my teeth [ding] a metal taste from the last [ding] post-funeral

church meal & [ding] that one was paper-plated & wafty napkins from piggly-wiggly

& all reminded me of eggs, grits, & south-carolina-sausage [ding] accurate nostalgia

& the difference between pumpkin [ding] & sweet potato pie [ding] is a lifeblood

[ding] & joy is a microwave [ding] & somebody's brother's ministry is logbooking

the menu at these things [ding] & he's *glad they fried the goddamn bird*

this time & it's fucking funny [ding] that

this time [ding] i agree

"History Never Repeats Itself—But It Damn Sure Can Rhyme"

after "An Open Letter from the Original Black Panther Party To Black (Hip-Hop) Artists Who Have An Interest In Our Community"

freedom knows enrapture, freedom as the contours of
wondering how we might make real
the interogatory's
sweat; freedom from being told we don't
understand, freedom to say
it's fascism all the way down; freedom
to say *fuck* when you see
approvingly
a Malcolm X quote
painted on a prison classroom wall; freedom
as beings
matted to a bedsheet; as being with yourself–
sticky with yourself,
angry that the only way you stayed alive
today was forgoing
the sun
light, water, cereal, bent spoon, touch
the answer in
the bounty of unwillingness:

21; freedom as intense culpability, as freighted possibility,
freedom as both. freedom as pyrrhic cycle
fractures, as not being—
get the predatory fear,
living within your years, as in, there is a way
out of no way. knowing no way
we make it this way again; freedom
to free our expectations, link
we forget,
to hum indiscriminately
indemning the disconnected sigh,
and undone by the heat of errantry
cooled by the heat of unremarkability
for the active unearning of sound
: the act of learning the side ways of silence
is lush entanglement; freedom *as*
forgoing; freedom as what keeps you up at
night; freedom, as the risk of knowing
that which never, we always, can choose

As the Prairie Burns

the fly:
It's in the hot-spring (the sulfur pool, the crude oil) where my leg kisses
my leg and I'm less alone for once. A mating dance with floating debris,
with my broken bits, with everyone else's scattered sense of time. My gadding
wings licking all this honey-coated warm, licking every winter still inside of me.
No matter how short your life, seasons come—

the fire:
What if you knew of everything that died the day they proclaimed you alive?
Borne of the yet-light, I wait, you call. I don't come unto terrains that do not
invite me. Martyrs do, unforgiving thieves too, but I sing the saint: sister-twigs,
mother-queen, I name the darkness, I am no king. I'm the feeling that this—*this*
—is nothing new. Now let me twirl for your indiscriminate touch. Let me be
and not be blamed when others bring you slick harm.

the fly, again:
I'm not lonely. Don't refute the company my shattered-glass coat brings.
I'm not lonely, I've got movement, I take myself to-go. I'm not lonely,
I love myself best when I'm left alone. I was left, see, and soon I'll go home.
I've got my living, I've got my wings, I've got my own heat. I'm grateful for it
all, but I've always been complete.

the flames:
To cut a body open is to recognize the body as closed. To abuse the ground
is to act as if it was not made of dry bone. To say *yes or no* to life is to imply
someone will ever ask. Move, lovely, through our hot undoing. What's the use,
sticking it out, when it's an empty world you roam? Trick question.
To clear a field, all you do is scrub, silt, and clean a place: again and again.

* * * **OF** * * *

Guilt By Association

How am I supposed to act around all this fight? Respond to dizzy

hornets, silly crabapple trees slapping smirks & eyebrowed delight

up on me—there is a daffodil threaded up in a shank of curl-sponged

hair. Apprehend this sunless afternoon. The such sweet glaze within

galloping hills of green clashing downstream; haughty

pedaling drops of music last night plowed me into a good sleep

—& take me serious. No matter how shortened my life,

my Uncle's barbecue exists & I had it; I was lawlessness: I was

brushfire, the bug bites, box braids, porkloins in the pavilions—me

myself, & I, make an adjudicatory scene. *So, call the cops. Do it. Go ahead,*

you've done it before, you've always been doing it, you're doing it already, don't you—

I didn't kill them. Just last week I found a crew of ants circling

a grain of rice that had leapt its way to the kitchen floor & I didn't kill said ants,

though I'm told I could've; I didn't kill them, despite their illegal enterprise,

& even still I didn't push the little invaders outside, where it's said they belong.

I didn't. Whose good am I responsible to? I blink *infinite susceptibility.*

& that triggers something in you, or so it seems. Here.

Those ants. This world, right? This one wherein my Mom buys four bags of Christmas

-blend coffee even though I won't be home till June. A barista grinds the beans knowing

no better—unaware the grounds won't be "fresh" when used—but, by grinding they are now party to a corruptive pursuit. Look, I won't explain the forethought criminal

nor rehash the snags of visual fear that constitute the carceral prism of public space. I

still don't know how to spend my life outside of debating whether or not I'm a yapping grave.

But tell me–have you seen a stripe-tailed scorpion try climbing out of a swimming pool?

I too am disturbed: contentment finds me, stupidly, immaculately, staring up,

out: into; down. I spend most hours of most days—& have nearing most

of the years of my life—not wanting to be alive. I don't know what to say.

On a metal park bench—a lawn chair by a river—I'm Vermont, Cincinnati; February,

June. A smile has parked itself briefly on my face, after the morning tears, &

this summer my mother expects to see me. She wants to tell me what door to exit

at baggage claim, hear me breathing as I buckle my seatbelt, watch me

the next morning drinking a hot drink under a hot sun, & her,

an accomplice to any tidbits of caffeinated glee.

Two Blocks Off-Broadway

lonely   shows up at his apartment
wearing clutter like a wedding dress—
like a hundred set pieces for a cancelled
show.   he positions clown faces,
disco balls, and a pearl white bombé chest
so they layer the apartment's walls.
                              begging the world
to eclipse   what is already gone.
that's the old bedroom, he says—pointing,
locating the only place here i'd call clean
            and full at the same time.
white noise   pressed against the walls
and how i miss you   for him
the vacated space, the ghosted stage
                        the now familiar scent of what's gone—

] to be his roommate in death [

yes, there is the scorched naked wood
beneath the blue kitchen cabinet, and yes too
the patent leather scuff marks left behind on
the train-tracked floors.   so-called testaments.
benumbed things that only confuse, that only
send him reeling—almost lost him once—into the
dusty,   into the paint peeled corners that never
change: the dark parts of a gaunt place
where men like us first learn to live—love
still just a funny shadow.   and so
            he pulls,   he yanks the curtains,
dims the faint yellowed lights. acts as if he
was the only one ever here.

Western Osprey

If nobody hears the soft call,
the presumptions of a sound and a bird die.

I can't make it easy.
There is a cost to learning every thing.

If I keep speaking, in lieu
of a glacial melt: I will stay a hollow rock, smooth.

There is a petrified forest that implies a paused morality.
But colors thump skulls there; this

       is the work, both bloody and aligned.

I'm trying to say that I'm thinking
if you hide forever, the walls will still be tall.

It's natural to want armor,
hard to love what you've had to forget.

Dear claimant of an underworld: where birds skid dirt,
and wooly animals cloud the sky—it's yours.

Your hour of feeling your cinderblock tongue.
There too is an entire forest of unborn, fat-

tailed sheep, weeping. They too invent
a galaxy of sound.

Portrait of Black Boy Not As Colonial Plaything

the subject looks for an object. violence looks for its home.
a little dog sits on the stoop. a man looks right through me.
the subject looks for the object. the object looks for a purpose
and finds one in him. the subject is also a man. the subject
is also me. the object asks: *so tonight, what'll i be?*
violence also asks: *how do you want me?* the subject tears
the filter off a cigarette. smoke and mirror-stage. the object
doesn't get the point. a man looks right through me. this
is the point. the object looks for his glass of merlot. violence
becomes me. a person uses me. phrases are objects too.
one need not be a man to make an object a subject and an
object again. i'm a beloved neckpiece. a real gold tooth.
the object asks: *is this all i'm for?* violence rearranges the living
room. now, the subject is seen right through. a foreground
is constituted by a background that nobody wants to see. little
changes over time. the object is time. violence hides in me.
whose furniture is this? it wonders.

the subject explains:
there are objects in me. all objects are mirrors. there are
mirrors in me. violence looks at itself. the subject frowns.
the mirrors steal the show. violence craves a way out.
violence is the furnishing when the furnishing is me. all
that's in the past, a man will say. *the past?* i say. *the past*

does not escape me.

Leftovers, pt. 3

& it's what the microwave doesn't do [ding] no wings brought back to flight

& [ding] i am still [ding] whispering the terms & conditions of forgiveness

into every bite & look [ding] yes fam, my fam [ding] there's chitlins

& *denial* [ding] *anger,* sure & [ding] spare me the process [ding] the first question

for a man in sheep's cloth [ding] is who he would be without survivor's guilt

& remember [ding]: whenever you hear a question, ask it from whom did it run

—breathing exercises are the bargaining [ding] stage, right? & [ding] *wait,*

these aren't grandmomma's placemats, you bought these new? [ding] & if i'm

no *guest or special case,* how can i prove i'm also not about this life? [ding] &

what's a death-wish but upset at the joyous cry? [ding] & i can't weep loud, though i need to,

so who is this healing really for? & [ding] jessie's getting out after twenty-years

& [ding] we're noisy amidst [ding] the new-new pandemic & back together

in the epidemics [ding] & another of ours is dead [ding] & i talk the difference

between pumpkin & sweet potato as if race is biology [ding] [ding] but i mean

to say that teri got laid off [ding] & martin has a tiktok where

all he does is scream & i love our noses & [ding] how unsafe safety

instructions can be [ding] & we're outside pat's church [ding] my plate of just

cornbread & half-eaten pie crusts [ding] summoning the flies [ding] &

we're not at anybody's house [ding] & i'm with my brothers on the porch out front [ding] in midwest-cloudy-april [ding] humid & too warm & [ding]

reliant on an inconsistent breeze & christ,

[ding] i want to sprint indoors & find my cousin [ding]

kayla, in the church kitchen, & ask her *who's that*

by the fridge [ding] the shadow telling the machine [ding]

stop:
stop humming so loud

Bank Account of Many-Legged Longing

Today, a beetle next to my foot
puttered slowly, so slowly entire
hours must have had their way

since said beetle broke my line of
sight. Help me steal a sentiment
from all my looped time. It has been

a year: a whole year watering my
loveless, slight slumber. How many
tiny voyagers must run through me?

I tried to get outside: I touched the
wood-paneled walls of the rooms
still awake in me. I took my hands

& feet with me, when I trekked
through snow. I want to have
a past. You know the saying: make

the road by walking. But what if
I wish to jet? To be in flight. I think
I miss him, I really do. But I miss his

leaving ten times more. At least then
there was a place to be; the not-really
numbered nature of our days. Days

that are plump with brutality, that are
brutal, slow. Make my desire anything
but an argument waiting to be won. It's

not like half this bug's life has been
spent in front of me. It's more like:
I happened to just be sitting right here.

& On My Good Days

for Frankie Knuckles, the Godfather of House

& on my good days, I'm that ready everywhere, pocketbook renegade
look good, get the good, every me. That kick an Apple off your teacher's desk,
every empty bottle of moscato, every yet-but-thing, every taste of
medicine that goes down; it's outlandish and it's me. No day for old countries,
this one's got a steel missile: always a sign of a violent ugly cold. Foreclosures
redundant as rain, baby, & on the good, inflation is because homeboy took
a knee. On my good days, my negro-knows it: a bloody bankroll always
filters in. I'm talking the end of empire baby, I'm enacting the end
of the World, the cornerstores are serving slices of grease and possibility,
so forever is tonight. I've laced up my kicks, painted our nails black &
emerald blue, & I'm that every me, building anew: already running laps
amidst these guilt-ridden blues. So, let's dance ourselves. Let them
dread being unable to forget us. For, on my good days, we be
that rhizome loud democracy. We're here cutting up our suit ties,
bottlecap sucking, seeing municipal sidewalks crack, throwing bottles of piss at CCTV,
& it's all good: the scuff mark on your Razor's aluminum frame match your sometimes
ashy feet. Laugh out loud, boo. It's me: play the juice box, iPod nano; glitch a livestream,
it's fever speculative lawn-green backpack me, & on my good days I'm there & fine.
Be up in fake news, capital gains, & when September ends
–the good & the days are on & on. Baby,
how perfect our present-continuous: how anterior our pollen-kissed future
how subjunctive the future because, yes, *baby wants to ride* but *the risk of
inaction* is a butterfly's fairytale, is PC-MP3 on our tongues, is the dissociation
station that kept the days in the good–in the *us,* alive. On my good days, a painkiller is
a Clinton in a bush, is an *outpost of tyranny,* is a Clarence only in name, & on
my good days we're in the millisecond land of a jolly rancher, the actual fallen
droplet of sweat that says we did it, we felt, baby, we fell in love because the buses
run on time in this town, because sweetheart, we showed up empty-handed,
raced & unmoored, & that's how we leave, met, and meet, my baby & me–
& hey. Hey.
When the world is a jackass walking down the street &
coming towards you, there's only thing to do–tell him: *bitch, it's done.
I'm good. I don't wear my body how I wear my body for the likes of you.*
Even if it's only in your mind, sweet one.
Even if you're eight, even if the mall cop at Coral Ridge Mall
follows you into Spencer's, tell him by doing whatever it is that keeps
you safe & always-good & in & of you—tell him:
Watch this all you want, my flesh is no political data on injury.

              & having been it &
        on the good, we ready? For it's time to go play some
       notes in our own God's house. No choke, nor fury, we'll play in
      that no man's land, where we're not choked in the street, where
     we'll don a crown to burn it all down, & we'll play the game
   where our lives are on the line but actually acknowledge the fucking line,
we're raunchy, we're righteous, we're down. & sure Jan we're down on one
until we're guaranteed our health, we'll ring-pop tax-break filial-equality,
  & still, on my good days I'm talking about kink & slugs. Not reaching
across the aisle, talking my *Romney Can't Dunk* sweatshirt from '08: it felt *nice*
  but not *good,* because, say it kids, "*a fascist dream is still a fascist dream,*"
so, let's summon imbrications of care. I'm talking spell-casters of inexplicability,
        I'm talking many-gendered mothers of *that there* &
            try it & you're worth that too.
    & on my good days, I'm talking about what we've got to do. Baby,
       it's Frank's *cayendo,* Boukie's deleted tweets, it's SZA &,
but, Janet's *CTRL.* It's us colored & queer firework-sketchbook baddies & boys,
after *Crash* (and also *Crash*), before *Moonlight* not after broke mountains:
loves who loved themselves out of the wrench of gendered ploys, us knight-
rioters, who found ourselves in chatrooms, as deacons of the dark parts of dark parks,
  who put whole dreams in the *Sandcastle Disco* of black Noah's Ark, who
  put whole sooners-rather-than-laters in each other's hands like pearls,
       who felt pedagogy in Martha and the Vandellas singing
Dancing in the Street, & takes any chance to say we just knew Marvin Gaye wrote it,
   but girls are the heart of a good city's sound, & on my good days
baby it's us. Unwise uncompromised sites, we, reverberate a nature presumed,
inching us to that place our feet have been telling us they already knew.
We'll just use the music and a good God will have it move on through.
For Brother Frankie loved us baby. Witnessed us kissing mask-to-mask,
heard us drive the children across state lines, ordained the day in the fight
    of us & good. Good what he saw because you can hear it: he said
      let the music use you. & you know this congregation sang,
        a-fucking-men.

Working Naked

Loons cascade
in the lake
for a nocturnal swim.
Once they start,
they're all in.
I
droop low,
low
in the waters
of singularity.
I turn my back,
on my back
not myself.
Back there, I say
is a stock
of bad history.
Silk-screen
thriller
with every version
of unexceptional regret.
Yes, my bedroom-
buckled knees,
yes, my
floorless afternoons.
Out of breath,
drunk, endlessly
falling.
Retreats from
every bright
moon.
But I dare to be
what I've done and
what I do.
I cannot look
in the mirror—not now,
not as the
archive
of other people's hands
and my blood-struck
eyes.

I cannot stop thinking
about
this,
about me.
I want to
shake
all my holdings out.
And I'm trying to start;
as loons
don't really sit—
they move,
they plunge
to swim.
So, my want:
a hot bed of needles.
My want:
to do more
than disappear.
I admit, I am
afraid these days.
Afraid
there won't be anyone
left to forgive.
Anyone else to stop trying
to hate.
Afraid to be the bird that
just drops.
But who ever
is ready
to just leave?
To just
anchor-
weight out a sky.

* * * Acknowledgments * * *

I am grateful to the editors of the following publications where, often in other forms, these poems first appeared:

- *Ash Magazine (Oxford University Poetry Society):* "Disappearing Act"
- *Green Mountains Review:* "Sovereignty" and "Western Osprey"
- *Assaracus: A Journal of Gay Poetry:* "I Lied When I Said I Never Had Dreams," "The Trouble With Angels," and "Two Blocks Off-Broadway"
- *Juked:* "[A]bsence is an [A]xiom"
- *Sixth Finch:* "to love through what scares you"
- *TENDER LOIN:* "Scorpions in Bethesda," "As the Prairie Burns," "Portrait of Black Boy Not As Colonial Plaything"
- *BOAAT:* "Demand"
- *Boulevard Magazine:* "Bank-Account of Many-Legged Longing"
- *Forklift, Ohio:* "Working Naked"

It's a gift that there are so many people I want to acknowledge and thank for making this chapbook possible: it's a problem, because I'm bound to forget someone or something, and nevertheless a gift that the love and support I've received is nothing short of a bounty. These poems are for Isaac, Carlton, Evelyn, Lacy, Louise, Harry, Steven, Derek, and all those who stay with me, holding my hands, despite not being here. Aunt Bonnie, Nichole, and Melissa, I love you and never find words that convey how much I learn from your strength, care, and ways of illuminating what is right, good, and beautiful. To my entire family (aunts, uncles, cousins), thank you for showing me that it's possible to stay. Mom, Dad, Matthew, Stephen: y'all are my truth, unconditionally.

Thank you to the slam community at Washington University in St. Louis—Aaron Samuels who brought me in; Inklings and WU-SLam which then made me want to write. To the laundromat of Johnson and the Vermont Studio Center: Jenny Molberg, K.A. Hays, Brenda Peynado, KT Duffy, Justin Wisner, Chekwube Danladi, Antonio Lopez, Noor Ibn Najam. Kelli Maeshiro, Andrew Johnson, Caylin Capra-Thomas, and Yalie Saweda Kamara, y'all been anchors. And Sarah Green and Meg Ready, thank you both for every part of you—you've continued to hold me and my whole heart. To Cave Canem—where to begin? All the faculty, staff, and fellows have fed the flame, but I have to thank those who, in one way or another, tended to this work: Cornelius Eady, Toi Derricotte, Dante Micheaux, Chris Abani, Evie Shockley, Robin Coste Lewis, Amber Flora Thomas, Janice Harrington, David Marriott, Tracie Morris, Frank X Walker, Aaron Coleman, Rage Hezekiah, Jessica Lanay, Maya Marshall, Dustin Pearson, Alexa Patrick, Julian Randall, Clint Smith,

S. Erin Batiste, Raymond Antrobus, Steffan Triplett, E. Hughes, El Williams III, Ed Mabrey, El Roy Red, Marwa Helal, Umniya Najaer, Saleem Hue Perry, Jasmine Elizabeth Smith, Ali Abdul, and Kristiana Rae Colón.

I don't know who I'd be without those who make me feel at home. Thank you for being in community with me as I've been and am. From when we entered each other's lives: Ola Abiose, Namita Dwarakanath, Mamatha Challa, Mahroh Jahangiri, Evan Linden, Ayah Abo-basha, Alyssa Mendoza, Rose McCarty, Diana Hill, Reuben Riggs, Sammy Lai, Jonathan Karp, Jenni Harpring, Jill Stratton, Jacqui Germain, Tayler Geiger, Laura April, Cameron Kinker, Seiko Shastri, Carrick Reddin, Laken Sylvander, Jordan Victorian, Michelle Winner, Jennifer Ibe, Andie Berry, Rachel Landry, Field Brown, Meredith Wheeler, Andrew Lea, Alexander Wang, Katherine Warren, Jessica Wamala, Alex Diaz, Jim O'Connell, Lindsay Lee, Khomotso Moshikaro, Paolo Singer, Charlie Tyson, Isabel Beshar, Suzanna Fritzberg, Courtney Wittekind, Seham Areff, Fadzai Madzingira, Aliyyah Ahad, Harry Pasek, Julian Gewirtz, Mailyn Fidler, Michael Davies, Rachel Harmon, Sarah Yerima, Robert Fisher, Angela Navarro, Hadleigh Frost, Russell Bogue, Derek Siegel, Wendy Sawyer, Valentina and Harissa, G.D. Harkavy, Emmett Patterson, Crystal Feimster, Kate Birkbeck, Michelle Johnson, the Iconicity, Minh Vu, my Stryker Sisters, Dustin Galvin, George Edwards, Raymond Fang, Liz Jacob, Ezra Ritchin, Kailyn Gaines, Rachel Talamo, Nketiah Berko, Brent Godfrey, Mark Firmani, Karen Sung, Ann Sarnak, Alyssa Chan, Michelle Fraling, Aaron Bryce Lee, Ali Murat, Alice Chen, Mitch Batchelder, Emma Pérez, Upasna Saha, Juan Fernando Luna León, Fernando Rojas, Bo Malin-Mayor, Natalie Smith, Talia Rothstein, and the Big Friendship crew.

Luke Stringer for attending to these poems at their last turns. Julian Gewirtz and Mikkel Snyder: thank you for the always-care you've put into me having my words. Georgie Morvis, I love you. Thank you for believing in this, in me, and being there, stanza by stanza, through the years. And Tabia, Tabia Yapp. You've made me feel possible—as a person, a friend, and artist—for so much of my life, and your care, support, brilliance, and love still feel other-worldly; you have always shown up for me with such generosity and intention. I'm so grateful for you, for the generative notes you've provided on countless drafts of literally every poem in here. Thank you for reaching out to the solar system and reminding me that I can reach too.

These poems, and any good they do, exist: my family, Mamz, MJ, T-Baby, Reubs, Sammy, Ev, JKarp, Kinks, Seiko, Rachy Rach, Mer, Seham, Fadz, Derek/mom, my NHV musketeers, Swift readers, and Writers' Room—I hope you know. I love loving you.

* * * Notes * * *

- Stanza 6 of "I Lied When I Said I Never Had Dreams" quotes the study, Pierson, E., Simoiu, C., Overgoor, J. et al. A large-scale analysis of racial disparities in police stops across the United States. *Nat Hum Behav 4*, 736–745 (2020).

- "History Never Repeats Itself—But It Sure Can Rhyme" is a quote from a June 2020 open letter written by several members of the Black Panther Party for Self-Defense, including Panthers like Jamal Joseph, a member of the Panther 21. A group of Party members organizing in New York City, the Panther 21 were arrested in 1969 and accused of crimes related to the planned bombing of police stations and the Queens Board of Education office. The Panther 21—after what, at the time, was the longest, most expensive trial in New York State history—were acquitted on all 156 charges. after the discovery that undercover police agents were the primary instigators of the plan. On the witness stand, one undercover officer confessed "yes" when asked if he had betrayed his community.

- "On My Good Days" includes quotes from "Baby Wants to Ride" by Frankie Knuckles (1987), a speech by George W. Bush (June 1, 2000) regarding the "risk of inaction" with respect to the use of U.S. preemptive military force, remarks by Condoleezza Rice (January 18, 2005) referring to "outposts of tyranny" being countries that the U.S. had deemed had "fear" rather than "free" societies, and the club mix of "Let The Music Use You" by the The Night Writers (1987).

- "Guilt by Association" riffs on Michel Foucault's call "to make ourselves infinitely more susceptible to pleasures" in an interview titled "Friendship As A Way of Life" (1981).

JOSHUA AIKEN is a poet and black studies scholar. A Cave Canem Fellow, his poems have appeared in publications such as *Apogee, BOAAT, Copper Nickel, G*Mob, Muzzle Magazine, Nepantla: A Journal Dedicated to Queer Poets of Color, Pleiades, The Rumpus, Sixth Finch* and *Winter Tangerine.* Joshua was named a 2023 Writer of Note by the de Groot Foundation, holds graduate degrees in History and Forced Migration Studies from the University of Oxford, was the Policy Fellow at the Prison Policy Initiative and the Researcher-in-Residence for Artspace New Haven's exhibition "Revolution on Trial." A Teaching Fellow with the Yale Prison Education Initiative and supported by the Point Foundation, he is a doctoral candidate at Yale in African-American Studies, History, and Law.

Printed in the USA
CPSIA information can be obtained
at www.ICGtesting.com
LVHW010740181223
766731LV00006B/401

9 798988 255727